LIVE WEL
EAT RIGH
FIND YOUR LIGHT

ILLUMINATE YOUR PLATE

CATARINA M

ILLUMINATE

YOUR PLATE

CATARINA M

ISBN: 978-1-960136-80-0

DEDICATION

In remembrance of the
ones that not only taught me
how to cook but also taught
me to love to cook.

Thanks to my grandmother,
Violet "Mama" Stearns,
and my mother,
Barbara Stearns Taylor.

**Special thanks to my fantastic
children for the support and
loving care they've always shown.**

**BK Blair for providing
many of his recipes &
Casandre Medel for her
creative input.**

CONTENTS

Introduction

It's been said that people love to eat! Most all occasions center around eating no matter what that occasion may be. Family and friends gather for holidays, reunions, celebrations, and even funerals. There's always an abundance of food during all types of gatherings. For the most part, food is a comfort. People eat to live... people live to eat.

It took me a long time to learn that difference as I'm sure it has taken many others to understand it as well. Food today is not the same as it was twenty, forty, or even a hundred years ago. Most of the time it's unhealthy, genetically modified, injected with hormones and antibiotics and so many other very unhealthy additives. But we have also learned over time that through many cultures and even "back to nature" types of eating can be very healthy and also extremely delicious.

Did you know that not only do we taste food with our mouths and taste buds, but we taste with our eyes? The first thing we do is see food, then maybe smell it, touch it and of course taste it. It affects the senses and we not only deal with food physically but it can also affect us emotionally and metally. This is what I want to achieve for you, the reader of this cookbook!

My intent is to take you on an adventure that will touch your soul. I want this adventure through food to help inspire you to think about health, both physical and mental. I want to fill your physical soul with great food and your mental soul with positive vibes and thoughts.

I was taught at a very early age how to cook and fell in love with learning how to cook and what to cook. My grandmother was a wonderful southern cook and baker who made me realize that this is the way you show love to family and friends.

As I have gotten older I realized a few decades ago that type of southern cooking, while tasting amazing, wasn't the healthiest way to live. So my new journey of health began. I had become ill with a disease that caused me digestive issues and also made me very overweight. My love for food was becoming my enemy and I had to do something about it. I started researching to get healthier and still be able to enjoy food. I realized that our food system and the way food was grown and processed had changed over the years since I was young. I realized it was time to rid my life of the bad food that was hard on me and I started eating a Mediterranean diet. It made my physical body well, I lost 110 lbs and this made my mental soul well also.

I decided eating healthy was best and helps our body in many ways, but I also missed the southern cooking that I had grown up with. So this is why I decided to make this cookbook. I have taken recipes from my grandmother's and mother's recipe file and tweaked them into healthy, mouth watering recipes.

This book is also filled with other recipes that I have found to be delicious and mostly healthy because I always tweak them into my own way of cooking.

This journey that I am taking you on will also be filled with positive sayings, advice, and much, much more because I want people to know that food is an adventure for your mind, body, and soul. It lights up your life in more ways than anyone can imagine. So use your senses to visualize, smell, touch, and taste everything that I have to offer in this book.

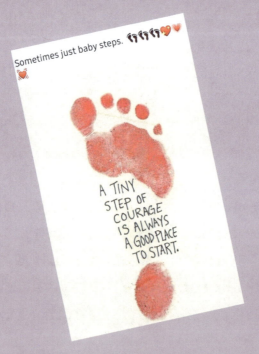

Enjoy life!!

Live Well...

Eat Right...

Find your light...

&

ILLUMINATE YOUR PLATE

If you're over 35 and want to defy each passing year while promoting a more youthful you... these 7 foods will help you stock up on some of the most powerful nutrients and you'll find them in the recipes in this journey.

- **Olive oil - Monounsaturated fats support healthly heart and also contains polyphenots, a potent anti-oxidant that helps age-related diseases.**

- **Red Wine - Yes, a glass of wine a day may have positive effects on health because of resveratrol content, an anti-oxidant that organic helps fight against diabetes, heart disease and memory loss.**

- **Beans - As you lengthen your years, beans have proteins that thicken and strengthen hair cells so you can lengthen your hair.**

- **Nuts - many nuts have a mineral called selenium. This helps slow down the skin aging process. A handful of nuts a day will give you benefits for anti-aging.**

- Tomatoes - Then are rich in lycopene. This supports healthy heart and cholesterol levels and is a natural sun block for protection again harmful UV rays.

- Raspberries & Blueberries - These 2 berries have anti-oxidants to help inflammation & stress that contributes to aging and wrinkles. Just one serving of these berries have more anti-oxidants than 10 servings of most other fruits and vegetables.

- Organic Eggs - Despite the bad rap eggs get because of their cholesterol content, which is based on completely erroneous science, eggs are rich in biotin and iron which help to promote healthy, youthful skin and hair.

Farm to Table

Appetizers

"BECAUSE GOOD THINGS COME IN SMALL BITES"

Eggplants

Catarina's Appetizing Egg Bites

INGREDIENTS

2T organic butter

1C sliced mushrooms

2T organic cream

1 clove garlic, chopped

3T shredded cheddar cheese

1/2C cut asparagus

1/4t sea salt

1/4t cracked pepper

4 large eggs

PROCEDURE

Preheat oven to 350 degrees. Fill 9" square pan halfway with hot water. Wipe olive oil in 4 ramkins, crack egg in each one. Add the ingredients as listed but don't stir, divide equally in ramkins. Put cheese on top. Put ramkins in the pan of water and bake for 18-20 minutes.

**Catarina's
Appetizing Egg Bites**

320 calories per cup

Scorpion Bacon Bites

Calories 69, Carbs 2g, Protein 3g

INGREDIENTS

1lb shrimp (16/20)   6 jalapenos
10 slices bacon   1/2C BBQ sauce
Best Rub - salt, pepper, brown
sugar, dark chili powder, paprika

PROCEDURE

1. For grilling or bake in oven 375 degrees.

2. Cut jalapenos 1" square, cut out center pith and seeds..

3. Butterfly the shrimp and season generously with the Best Rub.

4. Cut bacon slices in half & lay bacon flat

5. Place a jalapeno piece in the middle of bacon, and press down.

6. Place a shrimp on the jalapeno with tail up.

7. Fold over the bacon to cover shrimp and secure with a toothpick.

8. Bring tail of shrimp over top and secure with a toothpick to look like a scorpion.

9. Place the bites on grill or oven, cook for 25-40 mins until bacon is cooked almost crisp.

10. Baste bites with BBQ sauce and cook for additional 3-4 mins. Remove and serve.

Best Avocado Toast

INGREDIENTS

1/4t red wine vinegar   1 egg, fried
1/2t olive oil   2 slices whole grain bread, toasted
Pinch of salt & pepper   1/2 avocado, sliced
1/4C garlic hummus   1/4C broccoli sprouts

Best Avocado Toast
Calories 409, Carbs 40g, Protein 15g

PROCEDURE

1.Mix red wine vinegar, olive oil, salt, pepper and hummus together in a bowl.

2. Spread mixture on each piece of toast.

3. Top each piece with sprouts, avocado, and egg.

Proscuitto Wrapped Scallops
Calories 245

INGREDIENTS

1 1/2lbs scallops

1/2t italian seasoning

1 1/2T balsamic vinegar

Pinch of sea salt & cracked pepper

1 pkg prosciutto

1T virgin olive oil

PROCEDURE

1. Preheat oven to 350 degrees and spray a baking sheet. Cut the prosciutto in half lengthwise to have enough strips for each scallop. Wrap around each scallop.

2. Mix the remaining ingredients together and drizzle 3/4's over the wrapped scallop.

3. Place each scallop on baking sheet, leaving an inch between for even cooking.

4. Bake for 15 minutes turning the scallops after 10 minutes then bake for remaining 5 minutes.

5. Remove from oven and drizzle remainder of ingredients over and serve.

Mussels in Wine Sauce

Calories 173

INGREDIENTS

2 lbs mussels

1/4C water

1T unsalted butter

1sm onion, minced

4lg tomatoes, chopped

2 cloves garlic, minced

3/4C dry white wine

Salt and pepper to taste

1T minced fresh parsley

PROCEDURE

1.Scrub the mussels in cold water. Put them in a large pot and cover.

2. Melt the butter, add onion and saute for 2 minutes. Stir in garlic another minute, then add tomatoes. Turn burner on mussels to high.

3. Cook the tomatoes for 2 minutes, add wine, salt and pepper. Bring to boil for 5 minutes until sauce is a little thick. Stir in parsley, put on low.

4. Steam mussels for 6-8 minutes, until the've opened. Put mussels on serving plate and spoon sauce over each mussel. Serve immediately.

Serrano Ham & Orange Bites

Calories 265

Serrano Ham　　　　　　**Baguette Slices**

INGREDIENTS

2 oranges　1/4C chopped, pitted Greek olives
1/2sm shallot, sliced　　　2T fresh orange juice
1T olive oil　　1 baguette loaf, sliced 1in pieces
1T white wine　　　　Serrano Ham, sliced thin
1/4t salt and pepper

PROCEDURE

1.Toast baguette slices while preparing mixture.

2. Peel and cut oranges into small pieces. Place in a bowl, add olives, shallot, orange juice, wine, salt & pepper. Toss to combine.

3. Place a slice of serrano ham on each baguette slice and spoon 1T of orange mixture on top. Serve and enjoy!

Barbara's Cheese Ball

Calories 190 per serving

INGREDIENTS

2C shredded cheddar
2C shredded monteray jack
2C shredded Mexican cheese blend
8oz cream cheese
1T garlic powder
3T chili powder

PROCEDURE

1.Combine all ingredients except chili powder.

2. Roll into a ball, then roll thoroughly in chili powder to cover ball completely.

3. Chill in refrigerator at least 3 hours. Serve with crackers or cut veggies.

Catarina's Healthy Trail Mix

Serving size: 1oz, Calories 190, Carbs 23, Sugar 4

INGREDIENTS

3T sunflower nuts

1T dried cranberries

1T dried blueberries

1T dried cherries

2T pepitos (pumpkin seeds)

1-2T carob chips or mix

1T chopped walnuts (or nut of choice)

PROCEDURE

Combine together, place in airtight container and shake to mix. Enjoy

Spinach a la Queso

Per serving: Calories 171, Carbs 6g, Protein 7g

INGREDIENTS

10oz frozen spinach

1sm can chopped green chilies

1 jar chunky salsa

1 box (2-3lb) velveeta cheese

1 vidalia onion, chopped

1 can cream of mushroom soup

PROCEDURE

Mix all ingredients and cook on high for 2-3 hours in crockpot. Serve with chips.

For a "spicy" good time, add some jalapenos

Cheesy Hot Crab Dip

Per serving: Calories 170, Carbs 3g

INGREDIENTS

1/4C mayonnaise

6oz fresh or frozen crab meat, drained

1/4C roasted red peppers

1 4oz can chopped green chilies

1 5oz C shredded Colby Jack cheese

1/2t hot sriracha sauce

PROCEDURE

1.Combine mayonnaise, crabmeat, peppers and chilies in medium microsafe glass bowl, covered. Microwave on high for 2-3 minutes, stirring each minute.

2. Stir in cheese and hot sauce and microwave for 30 more seconds, until cheese is melted. Serve with tortilla or Pita chips. Enjoy

Mexican Salsa
Medel Family Recipe

2T serving: Calories 12, Carbs 3g

INGREDIENTS

3-4 red tomatoes

1/2 onion, chopped

1/4C fresh cilantro

1-2 cloves garlic, finely chopped

1-2 jalapenos, seeded and chopped

1/8 of a tomatillo

Pinch of salt and pepper

Juice of 1/2 lime

PROCEDURE

Mix all the ingredients in a salsa maker or by hand, mix well. It's better to put it in the refrigerator for at least an hour before you serve it. My family recipe, serve with tortilla chips and enjoy!

Bacon and Spinach Stuffed Mushrooms

Per serving: Calories 70

INGREDIENTS

8oz bacon slices
1C chopped onion
3/4C crumbled feta cheese
48 stemless button mushrooms
10oz pkg chopped frozen spinach, thawed
4oz cream cheese
1/4t dried red pepper

PROCEDURE

1.Preheat oven to 375 degrees. Cook bacon crispy and take 2t of bacon fat, put in skillet on medium heat. Add chopped onion, saute for 5 mins.

2. Mix bacon, spinach, feta, cream cheese & red pepper with pinch of salt & pepper.

3. Place mushrooms on foil wrapped baking sheets and spray mushrooms with a little olive oil. Bake at 375 degrees for 3-4 minutes. Then spoon the mixture into each mushroom and bake for about 25 mins.

Bacon & Spinach Stuffed Mushrooms

*It's the little things in life...
Like you come home from a
hard day's work & the leftovers
are still good or your favorite
movie is on. You have to smell
the roses and know that life is
so short that you have to grab
the positive while it's there!*

Food for thought

Love yourself because you are the only person who is with you for your entire life.

NOTE TO SELF

Today will be a good day

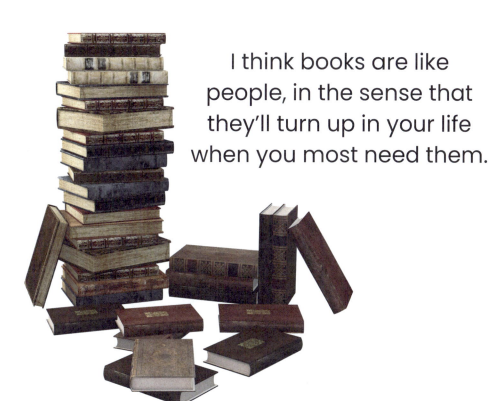

I think books are like people, in the sense that they'll turn up in your life when you most need them.

66

Don't close the book when bad things happen in your life... just turn the page and begin a new chapter.

Appetizers

"TINY TREATS THAT BECOME LOVE AT FIRST BITE"

All men should make coffee
for their women.
It says it right in the Bible...

"HEBREWS"

Coffee
PLEASE

Soups

AND

Salads

"WHERE VEGGIES AND BROTH MEET IN A WARM EMBRACE"

Green Chile Chicken Soup

Per serving: Calories 155, Carbs 5g, Protein 18g

INGREDIENTS

1/2C green chilies, diced
1T jalapeno, chopped
1 clove garlic, minced
1T onion, chopped
1/2t cumin
1t olive oil
6oz boneless, skinless, chicken breast
2T queso fresco cheese, shredded
2T mozzarella cheese, shredded
32oz chicken broth

PROCEDURE

1.Heat oil in a medium pan, add onion, jalapeno and garlic, saute for 2-3 minutes.

2. Add broth, pre-cooked chicken breast, cumin, green chilies and heat until almost boiling. Turn heat off and add chopped cilantro and both cheeses. Cover and let sit until the cheeses melt into the soup. Serve with french bread. Enjoy!

Stoyabed Stew

Per serving: Calories 235, Carbs 17g

INGREDIENTS

2lbs beef stew meat
1 can small peas
1/4C celery, chopped
1/4C green peppers, chopped
1 can mushroom soup
1 container beef broth
1 bay leaf

1C carrots, sliced
1/2C onion chopped
1/2t black pepper
1t sea salt
1/2C water
4 lg potatoes, sliced
1T garlic & herb seasoning

PROCEDURE

Put all ingredients in slow cooker on high 4-6 hours, stir half way through. Remove from slow cooker and serve hot. Enjoy!

Wild Rice Mushroom Soup

**Per serving: Calories 283, Protein 10g,
without meat**

INGREDIENTS

1 medium onion
3 medium carrots
3 garlic cloves
12oz mushrooms, baby bella
8C vegetable broth
1t garlic powder
1T each, dried thyme, oregano, dill
1/2C grated parmesan
1/2T soy sauce

3 celery ribs
2T olive oil
2T butter
1 1/2t sea salt
1/2t black pepper
1C wild rice
1/2C milk
1T cornstarch
Optional, add bacon or ham

PROCEDURE

1.Dice onion, celery, carrots, mince garlic and slice the mushrooms.

2. Add olive oil and butter to Dutch oven or soup pot, add onion, celery and carrot. Cook while stirring for 5 minutes then add mushrooms, saute for 2 minutes. Add garlic, stir 2 more minutes.

3. Add broth, wild rice, spices, salt and pepper. Bring to a simmer, cover pot and simmer for 1 hour. After 1 hour, stir in milk and parmesan. Add cornstarch stirring briskly until blended. Stir in soy sauce and anything optional. Serve hot & enjoy!

Greek Chicken Orzo Soup

Per serving: Calories 247, Protein 17g

INGREDIENTS

1C orzo pasta, uncooked
6oz pkg baby spinach
1/2C onion, chopped
2t fennel seeds, crushed
1/2t cracked black pepper
1C cooked chicken, shredded
4 cans (14oz) low sodium
chicken broth

4 eggs
1T olive oil
2T grated lemon zest
1t sea salt
1/4C lemon juice

PROCEDURE

1. Cook pasta per directions, drain. In large bowl, whisk eggs and lemon juice.

2. In large pot, heat oil on medium heat, add onion and saute for 3 minutes. Add broth, zest, fennel, salt and pepper. Bring to boil, reduce heat to low and simmer for 5 minutes.

3. Put heat back to medium, whisk in half of broth mixture to egg mixture and pour back into pot and cook while stirring until slightly thickened. Do not boil. Add spinach, cook about 3 minutes, stir in chicken and orzo. Cook for 2-3 more minutes. Serve and enjoy!

Shrimp Bisque

Per serving: Calories 270, Carbs 10g, Protein 24g

INGREDIENTS

1 1/2lbs medium-large shrimp

3T olive oil

2 cloves garlic

1/4C flour

2C half & half

2 leeks

1t each, sea salt & black cracked pepper

4T butter

1/4t cayenne pepper

1/4C cognac

1/4C dry sherry

1/2C tomato paste

PROCEDURE

1. First make the stock - put 4C water in pot, with shrimp shells, bring to a boil. Let simmer for 15 minutes, then strain the broth and add water to make 3 3/4C. Set aside.

2. Slice leeks and heat oil in soup pot, saute leeks for 5 minutes. Add the garlic, cook for 1-2 mins.

3. Add cayenne & shrimp, cook and stir until shrimp is cooked, about 3 minutes. Add cognac, cook 1 minute. Put mixture in food processer for a quick puree, set aside.

4. Melt butter in the pot, add flour, cook for 1 minute while stirring. Add half & half, cook until thickened. Stir in pureed mix, the stock, tomato paste, salt & pepper. Heat on medium, do not boil. Garnish with thyme or basil and enjoy!

Greek Chicken Orzo Soup

Shrimp Bisque

Keep your thoughts positive because your thoughts become your words.

Keep your words positive because your words become your behavior.

Keep your behavior positive, because your behavior becomes your habits.

Keep your habits positive, because your habits became your values.

Keep your values positive, because your values become your destiny.

It's said that we are
what we eat.......
so veg out and eat a salad

Parmesan Cheese
PLEASE

Best Pasta Salad

Per serving: Calories 290, Protein 8g

INGREDIENTS

DRESSING

1/2C avocado
1/4C mayonnaise
2T lime juice

1 garlic clove, grated
1/2t salt
1/4t cumin

PASTA SALAD

8oz whole wheat fusilli
1C cherry tomatoes, halved
1/2C frozen corn, thawed
1/2C cheddar cheese, shredded
1/4C cilantro, chopped
1/2C black beans, can
1/4C onion, diced

PROCEDURE

1.Dressing: Combine avocado, mayo, lime juice, garlic, salt and cumin in food processor. Puree until smooth.

2. Pasta salad: Cook pasta in large pot of boiling water per directions. Drain, rinse with cold water. Move to a bowl, stir in tomatoes, beans, corn, cheese, onion and cilantro. Add the dressing, toss and serve. Enjoy!

Mexican Chicken Salad

Per Serving: Calories 373, Protein 41g

INGREDIENTS

5C cooked chicken, chopped
2C Mexican cheese, shredded
1 lg red pepper, chopped
4oz green chiles, chopped
1/4C avocado, chopped
1/4C cilantro, chopped

1/2C sour cream
1/2C mayo
1/2C olives, sliced
Dash of salt
1/2C onion, chopped

PROCEDURE

Combine all ingredients and mix well.
Cover and chill for at least 1 hour. Serve
with tortillas or crackers. Enjoy

Mexican Chicken Salad

Steak Salad with Fresh Berries

Per serving: Calories 390, Protein 29g

INGREDIENTS

1 1/2lb flank steak
1T balsamic vinegar
2 cloves garlic, minced
8C romaine or butter lettuce

3C berries, any kind
2/3C terriyaki sauce
1/2C pecan halves
1t olive oil

PROCEDURE

1. Place steak in large baggie. Combine teriyaki sauce, vinegar, oil and garlic. Pour mixture over steak in the bag.

2. Close bag securely, turn bag over several times to coat steak. Refrigerate 2 hours.

3. Remove steak, grill for 5 minutes each side. Cut steak into 1/2 inch thick slices. Tear lettuce and put on 4 individual plates, lay steak slices on top, then put berries & pecans on top. Serve with Balsamic Dressing. Enjoy!

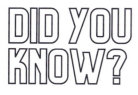

Iron-rich steak and vitamin C-packed berries in this salad not only creates a delicious flavor profile but also helps enhance the absorption of iron in your body.

Mexican Taco Salad

Per serving: Calories 331, Carbs 9g, Protein 20g

INGREDIENTS

1lb ground beef
1 avocado, cubed
1/2C gr onion, chopped
1 1/3C cherry tomatoes, halved
3/4C Mexican cheese, shredded
8oz Romaine lettuce, chopped

2T Taco seasoning
1/3C sour cream
1t olive oil
1/3C salsa

PROCEDURE

1.Heat oil in skillet on high, add ground beef, stir about 7-10 minutes.

2. Stir Taco seasoning into ground beef untl mixed well. You can add 1/4C water in with seasoning and let simmer a bit.

3. Meanwhile, combine all remaining ingredients in large bowl, then add ground beef. Toss together and serve with tortilla chips. Enjoy!

Catarina's Awesome Tuna Salad

Per serving: Calories 125, Protein 20g

Catarina's Awesome Tuna Salad

INGREDIENTS

1 can Albacore tuna
1/4C celery, chopped
1/2t parmesan cheese
1/4C kalamata olives, chopped

1t mayonnaise
1/4t garlic powder
1/4t parsley, chopped

PROCEDURE

1.Drain tuna, put in bowl and smash with fork.

2. Add the other ingredients to bowl, mix well. Then chill in refrigerator for at least an hour.

3. Serve with crackers or in a pita with sprouts as a sandwich. Enjoy!

Moroccan Couscous & Chickpea Salad

Per serving: Calories 343, Protein 9g

INGREDIENTS

1C couscous
1/2C dried cherries
1C boiling water
5T olive oil
1/2t ground ginger
1/4t ground cinnamon
3T rice wine vinegar

1 yellow bell pepper, sm pieces
1 lg onion, chopped
1 1/2t ground cumin
16oz can chickpeas, drained
1/4C cilantro, chopped
3T fresh orange juice
dash salt & black pepper

PROCEDURE

1. Place couscous and dried cherries in bowl. Add boiling water and cover bowl with plastic wrap, let sit for 5 minutes.

2. Meanwhile, heat 2T of oil in large skillet over medium heat. Add peppers and onions, saute for 5-6 minutes. Season with cumin, ginger, cinnamon, salt & pepper. Add couscous, then chickpeas and cilantro.

3. Whisk remaining 3T of oil with vinegar & OJ. Pour over salad, toss to coat. Serve & enjoy!

46

Rice, Pasta and Italian

"Why did the tomato turn red? Because it saw the salad dressing!!"

Just like an italian dish..... always keeping things saucy!!!

Italian Mushroom Pasta

Italian Mushroom Pasta

Per serving: Calories 278, Protein 13g

INGREDIENTS

8oz wheat fettuccine
6C Savoy cabbage, shredded
4 portabelo mushrooms, sliced thin
3 cloves garlic, minced
1C cherry tomatoes, halved
1C smoked Gouda or Cheddar, diced
1/4t cracked black pepper

2t olive oil
1 onion, chopped
2t flour
3/4C white wine
3/4t dried sage
1t sea salt

PROCEDURE

1.Bring large pot of water to a boil. Cook pasta about 4 minutes. Add cabbage and contiume cooking, stirring occasionally, about 4 minutes more. Reserve 1/2C of cooking liquid and drain pasta and cabbage.

2. Meanwhile, heat oil in large skillet over medium heat. Add mushrooms, onion and garlic, stirring often about 5 minutes.

3. Whisk wine and flour in small bowl, add to the pan with salt and pepper. Cook and stir about 1 minute, add tomatoes, cook 1 minute.

4. Return pasta & cabbage to pot, add mushroom sauce, reserved liquid, cheese & sage. Mix, enjoy

Baked Spaghetti

Per serving: Calories 350, Protein 22g

INGREDIENTS

8oz pkg spaghetti
1lb lean ground beef
1t dried oregano
1 jar tomato basil pasta sauce
2C italian-blend cheese, shredded
1/2t garlic powder

1/4C bell peppers, diced
1C onions, diced
3 large eggs
1t sea salt

PROCEDURE

1. Bring water to boil, add pasta. Preheat oven to 400 degrees

2. Cook pasta per directions. Combine beef, onions, peppers, 1 egg, oregano, salt & garlic powder in a bowl. Spread mixture in 13x9 inch baking dish.

3. Drain pasta, do not rinse. Whisk 2 eggs in bowl until blended. Stir in 1/2C cheese, toss to coat. Spread pasta evenly over meat. Pour pasta sauce over it and sprinkle with remaining 1 1/2C cheese. Bake 30-35 minutes & let stand 5 minutes. Serve and enjoy!

BLACK RICE

Also known as "forbidden rice" because only emperors were allowed to eat it, black rice may be the cheapest source of antioxidants around. According to the American Chemical Society, black rice has more antioxidants than a spoonful of blueberries, with more fiber, more vitamin E, and less sugar. More antioxidants means less inflammation, which means less fat storage for you.

QUINOA

It's a complete protein, meaning that it contains the complete chain of amino acids that are necessary for muscle building and fat loss. (Brown rice is an incomplete protein.) In a 2015 study in the Journal of Diabetes Investigation, researchers discovered that patients who ingested higher amounts of vegetable protein were far less susceptible to metabolic syndrome (a combination of high cholesterol, high blood sugar, and obesity). It's also high in the amino acid lysine, which helps you burn fat and maintain healthy bones and skin. According to a study published in the journal Food Chemistry, quinoa has the highest level of betaine, a chemical that revs your metabolism and actually shuts down the genes that encourage fat to hang around.

Shrimp Pasta for Two

Per Serving: Calories 700, Protein 42 g

INGREDIENTS

1/4lb fettuccine

1 tomato, chopped

2T basil, chopped

2-3 mushrooms, sliced

2T balsamic vinaegrette

1/2lb uncooked
large shrimp

2oz cream cheese, cubed

2T parmesan cheese,
shredded

PROCEDURE

1.Pour dressing over shrimp in bowl, refrigerate 25 minutes to marinate.

2. Cook pasta per directions, meanwhile heat shrimp in skillet over medium heat and cook 3 minutes, stirring frequently. Remove from heat.

3. Add tomatoes, mushrooms, cream cheese and 1T basil to skillet, cook & stir 3-4 minutes.

4. Drain pasta, place on platter, top with shrimp mixture, remaining basil & shredded cheese. Serve and enjoy.

Asparagus & Shrimp Risotto

Per serving: Calories 385, Protein 34g

INGREDIENTS

1/2lb asparagus

1 beef bouillon cube

1T olive oil

1 1/2C Italian risotto rice

1/2C Parmigiano Cheese, grated

Dash sea salt & black pepper

10-12 large shrimp

1T parsley, chopped

1/2C onion, chopped

4T butter

PROCEDURE

1.Bring water to boil, add 1T salt & asparagus, cover, cook 2-3 mins. Remove, set water aside.

2. Chop 3-4 shrimp into 1/2 inch pieces, rest of shrimp used later. Cut off tips of asparagus, set aside. Chop rest into 1/4 inch pieces. Add 3/4C water to asparagus broth, simmer & add bouillon cube until disolved.

3. Take large skillet, add 2T butter, olive oil, onion and cook 3-4 minutes. Add cut pieces of Asparagus, ALL shrimp and stir for 2 mins Remove whole shrimp and set aside..

4. Add rice to the skillet, stir, add 1/2C of asparagus broth. Stir until liquid has evaporated, add a cup of water, stir until rice is done, water has evaporated. Do not overcook or dry out.

5. When risotto is done, turn off heat and add 2T of broth, chopped parsley and Parmigiano cheese. Add touch of salt & pepper if needed.

6. Put risotto on a serving platter, arrange asparagus tips and whole shrimp over the top. Serve and enjoy!

Asparagus & Shrimp Risotto

Grilled Pizza

Per serving: Calories 259, Protein 8g

OPTIONAL TOPPINGS

Tomato sauce
Onion, sliced thin
Mushrooms, sliced
Cheese, mozzarello or
parmesan, shredded

Herbs, fresh or ground
Tomatoes, sliced thin
Pepperoni

PROCEDURE

1.Prepare grill for high heat. In a small bowl, put olive oil so you can grease the grate on grill & for brushing the pizza dough. (You can make your own dough or use crust, in a store already made) Prepare toppings to be ready

2. Grill one side of pizza only, place pizza dough on grill, close lid and cook for 2 minutes, make sure down side is brown. The top of the dough will start bubbling up.

3. Remove from grill, turn over so brown side is up. Brush with olive oil and add toppings. Keep in mind some veggies will be more crunchy, if you prefer softer, cook a bit before

4. Slide the pizza back on the grill, close the lid and cook for 3 more minutes or until cheese is bubbly. Remove from grill and let rest before cutting. Slice and enjoy!

Grilled Pizza

BK's Homemade Marinara Sauce

Per serving: Calories 54, Carbs 4g

INGREDIENTS

2lbs San Marzano Tomatoes
2.5T minced garlic
1T crushed red pepper
1/2C chopped green pepper
1/2C sliced mushrooms
1T fresh oregano
2 shallots, finely chopped

6T olive oil
2T fressh basil
1t sugar
1.5t salt
1t black pepper
2T tomato paste

PROCEDURE

1.Heat large pan on medium, use 5T of oil to saute the shallot, garlic, crushed red pepper and oregano. Also blanch the tomatoes for 2 minutes, put in ice bath then peel.

2. Blend in a blender with the remailing oil until smooth. Add tomatoes to saute and bring to a boil. Lower heat to a simmer, add remaining ingredients and simmer for 2 hours.

3. Spoon over wheat spaghetti or pasta of choice. Sprinkle with parmesan, serve with bread. Enjoy.

BK's Homemade Marinara Sauce

Today I plan on being as useless as the G in lasagna.

Surf n Turf Paella

Per serving: Calories 380, Protein 28g

INGREDIENTS

12 shrimp, peeled
12 small scallops
1C white fish, 1/2in pieces
1/2C fresh or frozen peas
1/2t saffron threads, crushed
1/2C dry white wine
1 chicken thigh, 1/2in pieces
1/4t ground black pepper

3 garlic cloves, minced
1C minced onions
6T olive oil
1/2t salt
1.5C grain rice
2-3C chicken stock
2 lbs mussels
2-3 lemon wedges

2 cans Italian style plum tomatoes, chopped

PROCEDURE

1.Heat 1/4C of the oil in paella pan or big skillet over medium heat until hot. Add shrimp, saute 1-2 mins. Remove shrimp, then add 1T of oil, add scallops, saute 1-2 mins. Removes scallops, then add chicken, saute for 3-5 mins until brown. Remove chicken.

Surf n Turf Paella

2. Add remaining oil, stir in onions and garlic, saute 5-8 mins, stir in tomatoes, add little salt & pepper. Add white fish, simmer covered, stir occasionally 25 mins.

3. Place wine in saucepan, drop 1 bay leaf, sprig of thyme, small amount of parsley and 1.5lbs of mussels and cook, cover partially for 3-5 mins. Make sure the mussels open. Remove mussels. Strain wine mixture into 4C container, add enough chicken stock to measure 3C.

4. Heat oven to 350 degrees, cut shrimp into 1/2 inch pieces, cut scallops in half. Stir shrimps, scallops, mussels, rice saffron, 1/2t salt & 1/4t pepper into chicken mixture. Heat to boiling.

5. Put pan on bottom oven rack, bake partly covered for 15 mins. Place fish & remaining mussels on top of rice, sprinkle with peas, bake until liquid is absorbed & rice is tender, about 10mins. Let stand for 5 mins, Garnish with lemon, serve and enjoy!

Chinese Long Noodles

Per serving: Calories 450, Protein 20g

INGREDIENTS

20 shrimp *, shelled
1/2C red or yellow peppers, cut small piece
1/2C green cabbage, shredded
1/4C green onions, chopped
1/2 sm yellow onion, strips
1/2pkg angel hair pasta
1/2C carrot wedges

Sauce Ingredients:

1t soy sauce
1T worcester sauce
1T sugar
1t oyster sauce

PROCEDURE

1.Combine all sauce ingredients together, set aside. Add small amount of olive oil to a skillet, cook veggies about 5 minutes on medium heat.

2. Cook pasta per directions. Add shrimp to skillet and cook for 5-6 minutes Add the sauce mixture for another 5 mins. Remove from heat and add pasta into mixture, Toss until noodles are covered. Garnish with Purple or green basil leaves. Serve and enjoy!

*can substitute beef, pork or chicken

60

Chinese Long Noodles

Why did the noodle go to the doctor? *Because it was feeling a bit twisted!*

Fried Rice with Shrimp and Broccoli

Per serving: Calories 418, Carbs 54g Protein 16g

INGREDIENTS

For marinade:

1/2t ginger , minced

juice of 1/2 lime

2T soy sauce

1T olive oil

1 clove garlic, minced

pinch of salt, pepper, red pepper flakes

For rice:

10 lg shrimp, peeled

2 carrots, chopped

1T olive oil

Juice of 1/2 lime

1/2 onion, chopped

2 broccoli crowns

1 egg

1T soy sauce

pinch of red pepper flakes

PROCEDURE

1.Whisk marinade ingredients in a bowl, add shrimp, toss to coat and set aside.

2. Add broccoli to food processor & pulse about 5-10 times until finely chopped.

3. Heat large skillet medium-high, add olive oil, onions & carrots, saute for 5 minutes until soft. Add red pepper flakes.

4. Add shrimp & marinade, cook for 3-5 minutes. Crack egg in skillet, toss with ingredients in skillet. Add broccoli, soy sauce & heat 1-2 mins. Squeeze lime juice, serve & enjoy!

Did you hear about the chef that died?
He pasta way
We cannoli do so much
His legacy will become a pizza history
He ran out of thyme

Food for thought

Self Love

When you love yourself, you glow from the inside. You attract people who love, respect, and appreciate your energy. Everything starts with and how you feel about yourself. Start feeling worthy, valuable and deserving of receiving the best life has to offer. Be magnetic.

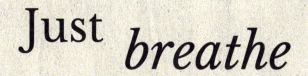

Just *breathe*

We fall.
We break.
We fail.

but then,

We rise.
We heal.
We overcome.

ALL IN
GOOD FUN
AND
GOOD FOOD

COOK WITH A SMILE ☺

WHAT DO YOU CALL A FAKE NOODLE??

HA HA HA HA HA

AN "IM-PASTA"!!

HA HA HA HA HA

The Fowl Group

Turkey Meatloaf a la BK

Per serving: Calories 216, Protein 28g

INGREDIENTS

1lb ground turkey
1/4 onion
2 eggs
1T cumin
pinch of sea salt & black pepper

1/2 green pepper
1.5C bread crumbs
1T paprika
1t cayenne pepper

SAUCE FOR DIPPING:

1/8C BBQ sauce
1C ketchup

3T brown sugar
Salt & pepper to taste

PROCEDURE

1.Start by putting the onion & pepper in blender or food processer. Blend until liquefied, then add all ingredients except 1/4C of bread crumbs. Mold into a loaf, cover outside with remaining bread crumbs. Bake at 400 degrees for 1 hour.

2. While the loaf is cooking, combine all the ingredients for the sauce in a bowl. When loaf is through baking, remove and cut. It should be a little crispy on the outside and great for dipping in the sauce. Serve and enjoy!

Food for thought

> 66
>
> Love yourself for all
> you have been,
> all you are and all
> you will become.

I think **books**
are like people,
in the sense that
they'll turn up
in your life
when most
need them.

Hummus Topped Panko Chicken

Per serving: Calories 510, Protein 31g

INGREDIENTS

1lb chicken cutlets
3/4C Panko breadcrumbs
2 boxes brown rice
3T cilantro, chopped
1t sea salt
2T honey
2t chili powder

16oz bag cut carrots
3T olive oil
juice of 2 limes
8oz jalapeno hummus
1t black pepper
1T water

Hummus Topped Panko Chicken

PROCEDURE

1.Season chicken with half the salt and pepper. Coat both sides of chicken with 3/4C hummus. Dip chicken into Panko crumbs on both sides. Cook rice per directions on box.

2. Preheat saute pan on medium, place oil in pan, add chicken and cook 3-4 minutes on each side until brown.

3. Combine remaining hummus with cilantro, lime juice, and water. Set aside.

4. Steam carrots in a steamer or microwave for 5-8 minutes until tender but not overcooked.

5. In a bowl, whisk together honey, chili powder, remaining salt & pepper until blended. Stir carrots into sauce. Pour hummus mixture over the chicken. Serve and enjoy!

Roast Turkey with Spinach Stuffing

Per serving: Calories 633, 66g protein

INGREDIENTS

6lb whole turkey breast, boned

5T olive oil

1C diced ham

1C grated parmesan cheese

(2) 10oz box frozen chopped spinach

1/4t ground nutmeg

4 garlic cloves, minced

1/2C bread crumbs

2 eggs, lightly beaten

pinch sea salt & pepper

kitchen twine

1/2C dry white wine

2C chicken broth

4t cornstarch

4t cold water

Roast Turkey with Spinach Stuffing

PROCEDURE

1.Heat 1T oil in skillet over medium heat. Add ham, reduce heat to low & cook 5 minutes. Add 1T oil and then the garlic, saute for 1 min. Stir in spinach, nutmeg, little salt & pepper, cook 2-3 mins. Transfer to bowl, stir in cheese and bread crumbs, stir in eggs.

74

2. For the turkey, heat oven to 400 degrees, cut 30in piece of kitchen twine, lay vertically on work surface. Cut 6 18in pieces of twine, lay across middle of long piece of twine. Center turkey breast, skin side down on twine. Season turkey with 1/2t salt & pepper. Cut small incision in top of turkey, place stuffing from bowl, then bring sides of turkey up around stuffing.

3. Tie turkey crosswise with the 18in pieces of twine, then lengthwise with 30in piece of twine to reinforce, snip off ends of twine. Coat heavy cookie sheet with spray, set turkey in center, skin side up. Brush with 1T oil, season with 1/2t of salt & pepper. Roast turkey 45 mins.

4. Go back to skillet you used for stuffing, turn on low heat. Add wine, stirring to loosen browned bits, add broth & simmer. Whisk in cornstarch & cold water, simmer until thickened. Take turkey out & transfer to cutting board, let rest for 10mins. Slice turkey & pour sauce over it. Serve with potatoes or your choice of a side. Enjoy!

Chicken Enchilada-Stuffed Spaghetti Squash

Per serving: Calories 408, Protein 34g

INGREDIENTS

2 chicken breasts, no skin or bone
(1) 3lb spaghetti squash
1.4C red endhilada sauce
1C jack cheese, shred
1 zucchini, diced

PROCEDURE

1.Preheat oven to 450 degrees. Place chicken in saucepan, cover with water, bring to boil. Cover, reduce heat to low 10-15 mins. Transfer chicken to cutting board, shred and put in large bowl.

Chicken Enchilado-Stuffed Spaghetti Squash

76

2. Cut squash in half lengthwise, de-seed and place cut side down on microwave dish, add 2T water. Microwave uncovered, for 10mins.

3. Scrape inside of squash into a bowl & stir in 1C enchilada sauce, zucchini, 1/2t of salt & pepper, add chicken. Mix well & spoon into squash shells, put on oven safe pan. Then top with remaining enchilada sauce and cheese.

4. Bake on lower rack for 10 mins, turn on broiler to high about 2 mins, until cheese starts to brown. Serve & enjoy!

Why did the spaghetti squash get invited to the party? *Because it heard there would be a "squash-tastic" chicken enchilada stuffing!*

Asparagus Stuffed Chicken

Per serving: Calories 288, Protein 31g

INGREDIENTS

2 med-lg chicken breasts
8-10 pieces of asparagus
1/2t garlic powder
1oz shredded mozzarella cheese

1/4t sea salt
1/4t black pepper
1T olive oil

Asparagus Stuffed Chicken

PROCEDURE

1.Preheat oven to 425 degrees, cut chicken in half, length-wise, leaving one side intact. (Creates a pocket to stuff). Season inside & out with garlic powder & half of salt & pepper. Put half of the mozzarella cheese & half the asparagus in the center of each breast and fold over, enclosing the filling.

2. Use cast iron or oven safe skillet, heat over medium heat, add 1T oil. Cook chicken top side down, for 3-5mins until golden brown. Flip chicken over & cook another 3-5mins to sear the bottom side. Carefully cover skillet with foil, place in the oven. Bake for 15 minutes, then remove the skillet and let sit, covered for 5 mins. Serve with side of red potatoes and enjoy!

"This chicken dish

is so good...

it's clucking amazing"

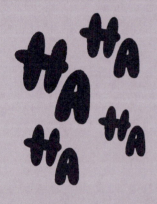

AFTER TUESDAY,

EVEN THE

CALENDAR

GOES

WTF

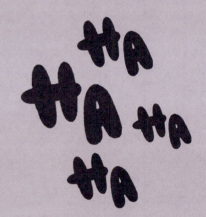

DAIRY SUBSTITUTIONS

Ingredient	Substitution
 **Milk**	Half-and-half or heavy cream thinned with water, evaporated milk, light coconut milk, light cream, oat milk, nut milk, soy milk.
 **Half-and-half**	Thicken milk with a little cornstarch or flour (about 1 tablespoon per cup of liquid) or thin heavy cream with a splash of water.
 **Heavy Cream**	For 1 cup heavy cream, use 3/4 cup milk and 1/4 cup melted butter, or thicken 1 cup milk with 1 to 2 tablespoons cornstarch or flour. (Whisk milk into cornstarch or flour little by little.) Coconut milk
 **Butter**	If using butter to conduct heat, as in pan-frying, use olive oil or other fats. For flavor substitutions, like butter in risotto or polenta, a number of creamy options like heavy cream or mascarpone will work.

Pineapple Chicken Huli

Per Serving: Calories 358, Protein 32g

INGREDIENTS

1C pineapple juice, unsweet

1/2C brown sugar

1.5t minced garlic

4lb boneless, skinless chick thighs or breasts

1/2C soy souce

2t fresh ginger, grated

2T cornstarch

Pineapple Chicken Huli

PROCEDURE

1.In a bowl, whisk pineapple juice, soy sauce, brown sugar, ginger and garlic.

2. Place chicken into a crockpot, pour sauce mixture over the top of them, cook on low for 5-7 hours. Then remove chicken from crockpot, whisk in corstarch to thicken sauce

3. You can leave chicken whole or shred & stir with sauce. You can plate it with rice if you choose. Serve and enjoy!

Turkey Mushroom Bake

Per Serving: Calories 372, Protein 35g

INGREDIENTS

6-8 pieces white bread, cubed
2C roasted turkey, cubed
(1) 8oz can mushrooms
1.5t poultry seasoning
1t sea salt
3.5C milk
10 eggs, beaten
1-2C cheese, grated

PROCEDURE

1.Spray 9x13 pan, arrange bread cubes, turkey, and mushrooms.

2. Whisk together the eggs, milk and seasonings.. Pour over bread, turkey & mushrooms. Cover with plastic wrap, refrigerate for 4 hours.

3. Remove wrap and top with cheese. Bake at 350 degrees for at least 60 mins, do not underbake. Serve and enjoy!

LIFE HACKS AND TIPS

HOMEMADE VICKS

- I Cup coconut oil

- Add 20 drops Eucalyptus

- 10 drops Peppermint

- Mix Well

- Scoop mixture in to Mason jar

- Store in a cool dry place

- Apply to feet and chest as desired

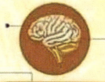

The Miracle That Is WATER
What does water do for the human body?

prevents loss of memory as you age

lessens addictive urges, including caffeine, alcohol and certain drugs

dehydration taxes the heart by causing it to pump faster to get sufficient oxygen to your muscles

water allows for efficient cell repair

water is essential for the body to sweat and release toxins

allows red blood cells to carry oxygen more efficiently, resulting in be muscular function and increased mental acuity

cleanses toxic waste from various parts of the body and carries it to the liver and kidneys for removal

without the flow of water there's insufficient water remove waste and toxins through your stool

lubricates joints and lessens discomfort from arthritis or back pain

s down the aging process and makes skin smooth

75% of Americans are chronically dehydrated

A University of Washington study discovered that one glass of water stopped hunger pangs for almost **100%** of studied dieters

The lesson to be learned?
DRINK MORE WATER

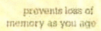
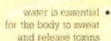

Baked Chicken with Peaches

Per Serving: Calories 185, Protein 35g

INGREDIENTS

4-6 chicken breasts, boneless
2 fresh peaches, sliced
1/4t cloves
pinch of nutmeg

1/4t ginger
1/2C brown sugar
1T lemon juice

PROCEDURE

1.Preheat oven to 350 degrees, place chicken in lightly greased 9x13 pan. Cover chicken with half the brown sugar.

2. Add peaches on top of chicken, then the rest of the brown sugar. Sprinkle the ginger, cloves & lemon juice over it, add pinch of nutmeg.

3. Bake for 30 minutes, basting occasionally. Serve with rice or your favorite side & enjoy!

Baked Chicken with Peaches

Thai Garlic Chicken

Per serving: Calories 324, Protein 27g

INGREDIENTS

400g chicken
breast strips

6 garlic cloves,
minced

1/2t crushed
red pepper

3T coconut milk
basil, for garnish

1/2T fish sauce

1T curry paste

1/2T brown sugar

1T olive oil

Thai Garlic Chicken

PROCEDURE

1.Pour oil in heated skillet, add garlic, saute
for 1-2 minutes. Then add chicken and cook
until brown, 5-6 minutes.

2. Then make sure the heat is low-medium, and
fish sauce, curry paste and stir well. Then add
brown sugar, coconut milk & crushed red
pepper. Stir and cook until it thickens.

3. Remove from skillet and serve over rice, add
fried egg & basil (optional). Enjoy!

Chicken Lombardy

Per Serving: Calories 389, Protein 32g

INGREDIENTS

8oz mushrooms, sliced
1/4t black pepper
1/2C chicken broth
1/2C mozzarella cheese, shred
1/2C parmesan cheese
2 green onions, chopped
6 chicken breasts, skin & boneless

4T melted butter
1/2C flour
1/2t sea salt

PROCEDURE

1.In a skillet, melt 2T butter over medium heat, saute mushrooms 3-5 minutes, stirring.

2. Cut chicken breasts in half, lengthwise and place between 2 sheets of plastic wrap, flatten to 1/8 inch thickness. Coat chicken in flour, cook for 3-4 minutes per side in 2T of butter in another skillet. Remove chicken when done, keep drippings.

3. Add mushrooms to skillet, add broth & boil for 1 minute, reduce heat and simmer 10 minutes while stirring. Add salt & pepper, pour the sauce over the chicken.

4. In a bowl, mix cheeses, onions and pour over chicken. Bake in preheated oven of 450 degrees for 14-15 minutes. Easy peasy, and delicious. Serve and enjoy!

Chicken Lombardy

Fish & Seafood

NOW STREAMING FROM THE DEPTHS

A Fin-tastic Bounty From the Sea!!

Creamy Spinach Stuffed Salmon

Per Serving: Calories 360, Protein 40g

INGREDIENTS

4 pieces of salmon
1/2C cream cheese, softened
2 garlic cloves, minced
1/2C parmesan cheese, grated

1C spinach, chopped

1/2t black pepper

SEASONINGS:

1t paprika
1t garlic powder
1t cumin

PROCEDURE

1.Cut slit or pocket 3/4 way through each piece of salmon. In a bowl, mix cream cheese, spinach garlic, parmesan cheese and pepper.

2. Fill each piece with the mixture, pack in good. Mix together the seasonings and rub on each piece of salmon.

3. Put salmon in greased oven-safe skillet, preferably cast iron skillet. Broil for 13-15 minutes until cooked to your liking. Serve with side of your choice & enjoy!

Creamy Spinach Stuffed Salmon

92

Blackened Swordfish

Per Serving: Calories 260, Protein 34g

INGREDIENTS

1.5lb swordfish steaks

2T olive oil

1/2t lemon juice

1/2t garlic, chopped

1t blackening seasoning

PROCEDURE

BAKE:

1.Preheat oven to 400 degrees. In a bowl, mix olive oil, lemon juice and garlic until blended. Coat both sides of swordfish with mixture, then sprinkle blackening seasoning on each side.

2. Place swordfish steaks in baking dish. Bake for 12-14 minutes, basting a few times. Serve with your favorited side dish and enjoy!

You can also broil 4-5 minutes or put on a grill 5-6 minutes each side if you prefer.

Shrimp Tacos Baja Style

Per Serving: Calories 500, Protein 23g

INGREDIENTS

1lb shrimp, peeled
2T cilantro, chopped
Juice of 2 limes
3T spicy ranch dressing
1 avocado, sliced
1/2C fish fry mix
2T mayonnaise
1/4C olive oil
8 flour torillas
2C shredded cole slaw mix

Shrimp Tacos Baja Style

PROCEDURE

1.Chop cilantro, comine with mayo in a bowl. Pour in lime juice (2T). Add slaw mix and toss to coat, set aside.

2. Mix ranch dressing with shrimp, toss to coat. Place fry mix in a different bowl, dip shrimp in fry mix to coat.

3. Preheat skillet on medium with oil, add shrimp and cook 3-4 minutes on each side until coating is golden. Drain shrimp on paper towel.

4. Warm tortillas, place avocado, shrimp and slaw in each tortilla. Serve with chips & salsa.

Baked Salmon in Foil

Per Serving: Calories 405, Protein 35g

INGREDIENTS

4 garlic, chopped
1/4t sea salt
1/8t black pepper
2t parsley, chopped
1/3C lemon juice
1/3C melted butter
2/3C parmesan cheese, grated
4 pieces of salmon, skinless
25-30 pieces of asparagus
Parsley sprig &
2 slices of lemon for garnish

Baked Salmon in Foil

PROCEDURE

1.Preheat over to 400 degrees. Place salmon in center of 12x18 inch sheet of foil, each.

2. Divide asparagus into equal parts and place them around the salmon.

3. In a bowl, mix butter, lemon juice, garlic and parsley and pour over salmon and asparagus.

4. Season with salt and pepper and cover all of them with the parmesan cheese. Bake for 20-25 minutes. Serve with rice and enjoy!

Garlic Butter Scallops with Lemon

INGREDIENTS

28oz raw scallops
3T butter
1/2C dry white wine
4t lemon juice
1/4C parsley, chopped

1T olive oil
3 garlic cloves, minced
1/2t sea salt
1/2t black pepper

PROCEDURE

1.Heat olive oil in skillet over medium heat, add scallops , single layer in pan. Season with salt and pepper. Cook for 2-3 minutes on one side for golden crust. 2-3 minutes on other side for same result. Remove from skillet.

2. Melt 2T of the butter in that skillet, stir. Add garlic and cook for 1 minute. Pour in wine and bring to a simmer for 2 minutes, until reduced. Stir in remaining butter & lemon juice.

3. Remove skillet from heat, add scallops back into pan to warm. Garnish with parsley and serve over steamed vegetables. Serve & enjoy!

Garlic Butter Scallops with Lemon

Awesome Spicy Crab Cakes

Per Serving: Calories 154, Protein 12g

INGREDIENTS

2-3oz crabmeat
2 dashes Tabasco sauce
2/3C wheat thins, crushed
1 red pepper, finely chopped
Pinch salt & pepper
5-6 green onions, finely chopped

2T worcestershire sauce
3T lemon juice
3T spicy mustard
3-4t olive oil
1C mayonnaise
2 eggs

Awesome Spicy Crab Cakes

PROCEDURE

1.Heat a skillet with 2t of olive oil and saute the peppers and onions. In a bowl, mix crabmeat, mustard, mayo, lemon juice, worcestershire sauce and Tabasco sauce. Add cooked peppers and onions.

2. In separate bowl, beat eggs and fold into other mixture. Add Wheat Thins, but don't make it bready. Add salt & pepper to taste.

3. Mold into 2 inch patties & put in skillet with oil, cook on medium until golden brown. Drain and serve with cocktail or tartar sauce. Enjoy!

When in doubt..... just crab walk away!!

Air Fried Salmon Bites

Per Serving: Calories 161, Protein 22g

INGREDIENTS

1lb salmon filet

3T tamari or soy sauce

2 garlic cloves, minced

1t sesame oil

Juice of half lime

1T avocado oil

1T honey

1T rice vinegar

1/2t minced ginger

PROCEDURE

1.Cut salmon into 1 inch cubes. Then whisk all ingredients together in a bowl. Add the cubed salmon, toss to coat and let marinate for 30 minutes to an hour.

2. When ready to cook, preheat air fryer to 400 degrees and place salmon cubes in single layer on flat sheet.

3. Cook for 7-9 minutes, flipping each piece halfway through. Serve with your favorite side dishes or with a dipping sauce. Enjoy!

Why was the salmon blushing at dinner? *It saw the lime sauce and realized it was getting a little too tart-y!*

Food for thought

Attract what you expect, reflect what you desire, become what you respect, mirror what you admire

TODAY
is yours to conquer.

A bird sitting on a tree
is never afraid of the branch
breaking, because her trust
is not on the branch
but on it's own wings.

Always believe in yourself.

Garlic Fish with Mushrooms and Broccoli

Per Serving: Calories 251, Protein 37g

INGREDIENTS

1-2lbs grouper or mahi-mahi   4T olive oil
2 garlic cloves, chopped   juice of 1 lemon
3/4C Chardonnay wine   pinch garlic powder
1C fresh mushrooms, sliced   1/4t dill

PROCEDURE

1.Preheat oven to 420 degrees. Then heat garlic and 3T of oil in baking dish about 3-4 minutes Sprinkle garlic powder and dill on both sides of the fish, put in the baking dish.

2. Place the broccoli and mushrooms on top of the fish, drizzle rest of olive oil over veggies. Add the wine to the dish, bake for 15-20 minutes until veggies are little crisp, but not mushy.
3. Take out of the oven, serve over Rice pilaf, quinoa or your favorite pasta. Serve & enjoy!

Beef and the other Meat

"SIZZLE THROUGH THE EPIC JOURNEY OF YOUR FAVORITE MEATS"

Rib Eye Steak Reverse Seared

Rib Eye Steak Reverse Seared

Per Serving: Calories 230, Protein 35g

INGREDIENTS

STEAK RUB:

1/4C pink himalayan salt
1/4C black pepper
1T chili powder

2T garlic
2.5T paprika

CHIMICHURRI:

1/2C parsley
1T dried oregano
1 shallot, diced
3T red wine
2/3C olive oil

1/4C cilantro
5 cloves garlic, minced
1t sea salt
1/2t black pepper

2 ribeye steaks

PROCEDURE

1.Drizzle olive oil over the steaks. Mix all of the ingredients for the steak rub and sprinkle it on both sides of the steaks.

2. Grill your steaks 5-6 minutes each side (or however you like it cooked). Mix the chimichurri ingredients together and pour over steaks after they have cooked. Serve with your favorite side. Enjoy!

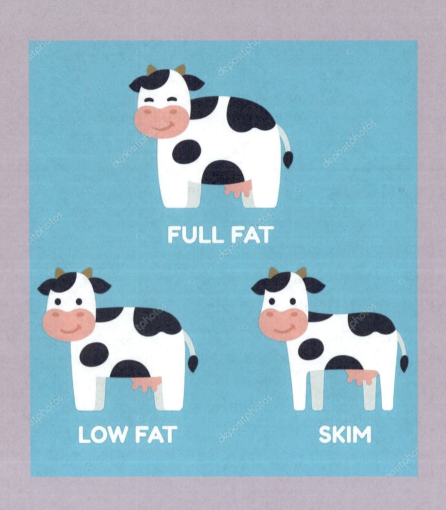

STEAK NIGHT

Grandma's Special Herbs

ROSEMARY

Sage Pork Chops With Apples

Per Serving: Calories 371, Protein 33g

INGREDIENTS

SEASONINGS:

1t minced garlic

1/2t ground allspice

4 boneless pork chops

1t sea salt

1 onion, sliced thin

1/2C apple juice

1.5t rubbed sage

1t thyme

1/2t paprika

1T flour

2T olive oil

2 red apples, slice thin

1T brown sugar

PROCEDURE

1. Mix flour, all the seasonings, salt in a bowl. Sprinkle both sides of pork chops with 1t of the mixture.

2. Cook pork chops in oil in skillet on medium until both sides are browned. Remove from skillet. Add onion and cook for 3 minutes, add apples and cook for 2 minutes while stirring.

3. Stir in juice, sugar and remaining flour mixture. Return pork chops to skillet, bring to a boil. Reduce heat to low, cover & simmer for 5-7 minutes until done. Serve with side dish & enjoy!

COOK WITH A SMILE ☺

I've got way too much thyme on my hands.

Oriental Beef Stir Fry

Per Serving: Calories 255, Protein 22g

INGREDIENTS

1lb sirloin steak

10oz beef broth

(1) 10oz pkg snow peas

1 garlic clove, minced

1C sliced mushrooms

(1) 7oz can sliced water chestnuts

4 green onions

1T cornstarch

1T soy sauce

2C broccoli, chopped

2t olive oil

Oriental Beef Stir Fry

PROCEDURE

1.Cut steak to thin slices, green onions to 1 inch pieces. Mix broth, cornstarch & soy sauce in a bowl, mix cornstarch until dissolved. Set aside.

2. Heat oil in a skillet or wok over medium heat. Add steak & garlic, stir fry for 3-4 minutes or browned. Remove with slotted spoon.

3. Add rest of the veggies to skillet, stir fry for 3 minutes. Return steak to skillet, add broth to skillet, cook stirring 3 minutes until thickened. Serve over rice & enjoy!

"This beef stir fry is so delicious... it's wok-ing my world!"

Asian Skillet Pork and Noodles

INGREDIENTS

2 carrots, peeled
1.5C green onions, sliced
2T sesame oil
1T olive oil
4 pkg ramen noodles, oriental flavor

2lb pork tenderloins
1 red bell pepper
2T Asian seasoning mix
4C water

PROCEDURE

1. Cut carrots, bell pepper into thin strips. Add sliced green onions. Slice tenderloins into 4 strips, lengthwise, then thinly crosswise.

2. Combine pork, sesame oil, seasoning mix & 2 of the ramen seasoning pkg in bowl, mix well. Add oil to skillet over medium & add half of the pork, cook for 2-3 minutes, stirring. Remove pork. Repeat with remaining pork

3. Add carrots & bell pepper to skillet, cook 1-2 minutes. Add water & rest of ramen seasoning, stir. Add ramen noodles & green onions. Cover, bring to boil 4-5 minutes. Add pork, stir & let stand for 3-4 minutes. Serve & enjoy!

Beer Infused Sausage and Peas

Per Serving: Calories 409 Protein 15g

INGREDIENTS

1 green pepper, diced
1C mushrooms, sliced
1T worcestershire sauce
2 cans blackeyed peas
1 can Rotelle tomatoes

1/2 onion, diced
1/2 can beer
1/2t garlic salt
1/4t black pepper
1lb sausage or kielbasa

PROCEDURE

1.In a skillet, add beer, saute green pepper, onion and mushrooms. Boil & reduce heat, then add sausage, worcestershire sauce, salt & pepper. Cook for 10 minutes
2. Drain liquid from skillet, add blackeye peas, and tomatoes and simmer for 5-10 minutes. Serve with rice or side dish of choice. Enjoy!

Beer Infused Sausage and Peas

Food for thought

-Grapes must be crushed to make wine.

-Diamonds form under pressure.

-Olives are pressed to release oil.

-Seeds grow in darkness.
Whenever you feel crushed, under pressure, pressed, or in darkness, you're in a powerful place of transformation.

Trust the process.

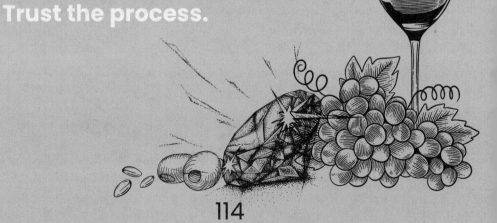

No one is you and that is your power.

Be who you are
and say what you feel
because those who mind
don't matter and those who
matter don't mind.

Greek Stew with Lamb

Per Serving: Calories 365, Protein 20g

INGREDIENTS

1lb lamb shoulder chops   2T olive oil
1 onion, chopped   3 garlic cloves, minced
1/2C dry red wine   2C tomatoes, chopped
15oz can tomato sauce   1/2 lemon, juiced
1/2t dried oregano   1/2t ground cinnamon
1 bay leaf   1C lamb stock
1/4C parsley, chopped   1lb fresh green beans
pinch Sea salt, black pepper

Greek Stew with Lamb

DID YOU KNOW?

Greek stew with lamb is a savory delight that's slow-cooked to perfection, bringing the flavors of Greece right to your table!

PROCEDURE

1.Heat oil in heavy pot over medium heat. Then season lamb with salt & pepper, add to pot, cook until browned (5 minutes) on each side. Stir in onions & garlic, cook about 2 minutes.

2. Pour wine into pot and bring to a boil, stir & scrape bits off bottom of pot. Stir in tomatoes, tomato sauce, lamb stock, lemon juice, oregano, cinnamon & bay leaf.

3. Bring back to boil over high heat, then reduce to medium, cover and simmer until lamb is very tender, about 1 & 1/2 hours. Stir in the green beans & cook until tender, 20 additional mins.

4. Remove bay leaf, garnish stew with chopped fresh parsley. Serve over rice or orzo & enjoy!

Food for thought

Good things come to
those who Believe,
Better things come
to those who are
Patient and
the best Things come
to those who
Don't Give up.

Potatoes and Veggies

VEGETABLES ARE NATURE'S WAY

OF SAYING *'EAT YOUR COLORS'*

Party Potatoes

Per Serving: Calories 310, Protein 10g

INGREDIENTS

12oz hash browns
1 can cream of potato soup
1/2C green onions, chopped
1C cheddar cheese, grated

8oz sour cream
1t sea salt
1/2t pepper

PROCEDURE

1.Mix together all ingredients except the cheese and put in a casserole dish. Sprinkle cheddar cheese on top.

2. Bake at 325 degrees for 1 hour until cheese is golden brown. Remove and serve. Enjoy!

Party Potatoes

Why don't potatoes make good friends?
They always got off to a bad starch.

Corn with Seasoned Cilantro

Per Serving: Calories 21, Protein 3g

INGREDIENTS

3C cut corn or canned
1/4C cilantro, chopped
1/4t cumin seeds
1 tomato, seeded & chopped

1/4C water
1/4t sea salt
1/8t black pepper

Corn with Seasoned Cilantro

PROCEDURE

1.Combine corn, water, cilantro, cumin, salt & pepper in a 2 quart baking dish, stir well. Cover with wax paper & microwave on high 6-8 mins. 2. Stir in tomato, cover again & microwave on high 1-2 mins until corn is tender. Add a little more salt & pepper if needed. Serve & enjoy!

Cheesy Broccoli Casserole

Per Serving: Calories 280, Protein 21g

INGREDIENTS

2 pkg frozen chopped broccoli   1/2t sea salt
1C salad dressing (or mayo)   2 eggs, beaten
1C sharp cheddar cheese   1T minced onions
1 can cr of mush soup   1/4t black pepper
1C ritz crackers, crushed

PROCEDURE

1.Cook broccoli in pot for 10 minutes, and drain.

2. Mix broccoli and salad dressing, eggs, soup, onions in a buttered or sprayed casserole dish. Cover with crushed ritz crackers & a little butter.

3. Bake at 350 degrees for 45 minsutes. Take out of oven, Serve and enjoy!

Cheesy Broccoli Casserole

COOK WITH A SMILE :)

Looks like a very serious leak under the sink

LIFE HACKS AND TIPS

In a process known as "companion planting," some plants are grown together to benefit each other. For instance, planting basil near tomatoes can enhance the flavor of the tomatoes and help repel certain pests. This technique has been used for centuries to improve crop health and yields in gardens.

Perfectly Roasted Vegetables

1. Preheat the oven to 450 degrees F

2. Cut the veggies and toss with olive oil and seasoning

3. Transfer them to a baking sheet. Roast!

White potatoes
35 - 40 mins
Best with oregano, thyme, and garlic

Broccoli
20 - 25 mins
Best with citrus zest, rosemary or thyme

Bell peppers
25 - 30 mins
Best with while cilantro, thyme, and parsley

Carrots
25 - 30 mins
Best with dill, parsley, and tarragon

Cauliflower
25 - 30 mins
Best with garlic, thyme and rosemary

Onions
25 - 30 mins
Best with basil, oregano, sage, tarragon, and thyme

Tomatoes
30 - 35 mins
Best with while basil, cilantro, and oregano

Asparagus
12 - 15 mins
Best with lemon balm, dill, and tarragon

Butternut squash
20 - 25 mins
Best with rosemary, thyme, and sage

Roasting vegetables not only enhances their flavor but also brings out their natural sweetness! It also retain more nutrients making them a healthy and tasty addition to any meal.

Mediterranean Quinoa Bowl

Per Serving: Calories 422, Protein 19g

INGREDIENTS

3C cooked quinoa 2 cucumbers, thinly sliced
2 avocados, diced 1/2C red onion, diced
1/2 red pepper diced 1t smoked paprika
pinch cayenne pepper 1/2t ground cumin
1C cherry tomatoes, halved
1.5C cooked chickpeas, drained
yogurt or Tahini sauce, drizzle

PROCEDURE

1.Cook quinoa per dirctions. Preheat oven to
425 degrees, line baking sheet with
parchment paper. Place chickpeas on
baking sheet.

2. Drizzle olive oil, sprinkle smoked paprika,
cumin, salt & cayenne on chickpeas. Spead
evenly on the baking sheet. Roast for 20-30
minutes until brown & crisp.

3. Assemble bowls with quinoa, chickpeas,
cucumbers, tomatoes avocado. Top with
onions, parsley, and red peppers. Drizzle
yogurt or tahini, serve & enloy!

Mediterranean Quinoa Bowl

COOK
WITH
A SMILE

"HOW DO YOU FIX A BROKEN TOMATO?"

TOMATO PASTE!!

Spaghetti Squash with Broccoli

Per Serving: Calories 194, Protein 12g

INGREDIENTS

2-3lb spaghetti squash, cut lengthwise, seeded

1C brocolli, chopped

4 garlic cloves, minced

1C mozzarella cheese, shredded

1/4C parmesan cheese, chredded

1/2t sea salt

1T olive oil

3/4t italian season

2T water

1/4t black pepper

PROCEDURE

1.Preheat oven to 450 degrees. Place squash cut side down, in microwave safe dish, add water. Microwave about 10mins, uncovered.

2. Heat oil in a skillet on mediium, add broccoli, garlic and cook 2 minutes. Add water, cook & stir till broccoli is cooked your way, 3-5 mins. Transfer to a bowl.

3. Scrape squash into bowl, put shells in a baking pan. Stir 3/4C mozzarella, 2T parmesan, italian season, salt & pepper into squash mixture. Put in shells, top with rest of the cheeses. Bake 10 mins, then put under broiler till cheese is brown. Serve & enjoy!

Spaghetti Squash with Broccoli

Sweet Potato & Pecan Crumble Casserole

Per Serving: Calories 290, Protein 4g

INGREDIENTS

5 lg sweet potatoes   1/2C butter
1C crushed graham crackers   1/2t sea salt
1C pecans, chopped   1t ground cinnamon
1/2C packed brown sugar   1/4t black pepper

PROCEDURE

1.Preheat oven to 350 degrees. Microwave potatoes for 18-20 minutes, altogether. While they're cooling, melt 5T of butter, combine with graham crackers, pecans, brown sugar & cinnamon in bowl. Set aside.

2. Peel sweet potatoes, put in a bowl & mash with 3T butter, salt & pepper. Spoon sweet potato mixture into a casserole dish, top with pecan mix.

3. Bake for 20-25 minutes until topping is golden brown. Serve and enjoy!

"Bring a veggie tray" they said!!

HA HA HA HA HA HA

131

When you are cooking, see your spoon as a wand and stir your intentions into what you bake.

@MyWitches1111

132

Desserts

"DESSERT IS THE SWEETEST FORM OF SELF-CARE"

There's
ALWAYS
room for
DESSERTS
it's
located in a
separate
stomach!!

Mama Stearns' Awesome Chess Pie

Per Serving: Calories 242, Protein 3g

INGREDIENTS

4 eggs, beaten
2C sugar
2T flour
1 unbaked pie shell

1 stick melted butter
2t vanilla
1C buttermilk

PROCEDURE

1.Preheat oven to 350 degrees. Mix eggs, butter, sugar, vanilla, flour, and buttermilk until blended.

2. Pour into an unbaked pie shell and bake for one hour or until knife comes out clean.

3. Cut into pieces, serve and Enjoy!

Mama Stearns Awesome Chess Pie

Pumpkin Muffins

Per Serving: Calories 155, Protein 2g

INGREDIENTS

2.5C flour
1T baking powder
1/2t ground nutmeg
1C pumpkin, not pie filling
6T melted butter
2/3C roasted pumpkin seeds
1/3C golden raisins, optional

1C packed brown sugar
1t ground cinnamon
1/2t ground ginger
1/4t sea salt
3/4C milk
2 eggs

PROCEDURE

1.Preheat oven to 400 degrees, grease 18 cou nt muffin pan or use paper baking cups.

2. Combine flour, brown sugar, baking powder, cinnamon, nutmeg, ginger & salt in bowl. Stir pumpkin, milk, eggs, & butter in another bowl. Stir pumpkin mixture into flour mixture until all are moistened. Stir in 1/3C pumpkin seeds & raisins (if using).

3. Spoon into muffin cups, fill 2/3rds full. Then sprinkle remaining pumpkin seeds over each one. Bake 15-18 minures until toothpick inserted & comes out clean. Cool 10 mins, Enjoy!

<u>Pumpkin Muffins</u>

Once you lick the
frosting off a cupcake,
it becomes a muffin
and muffins are healthy!
(You're welcome)

Mama Stearns' Jam Cake

Per Serving: Calories 570

INGREDIENTS

1C butter
6 eggs, beaten
2t baking soda
2t cinnamon
2t allspice
2C raisins
1t salt
2C sugar
1C buttermilk
4.5C flour, sifted
2t ground cloves
1t nutmeg
2C blakberry jam
1C apple butter

Mama Stearns Jam Cake

PROCEDURE

1.Cream butter, sugar & eggs. Sift flour, soda, cinnamon, cloves, allspice, nutmeg and salt. Add to the creamy mixture in the mixer.

2. Add buttermilk into the mixer, then the apple butter, mix until smooth. Add the raisins & jam, mix by hand until thoroughly mixed.

3. Pour into 3-4 round pans, bake at 350 degrees for 30 minutes. Let cool completely and ice with Caramel icing (either homemade or can) Enjoy!

138

Food for thought

You won't care "how long" it took when it shows up, remember that. Persist persist persist because it's already yours.

INVEST

in

YOURSELF

you can afford it. trust me.

Healthy Everything Cookies

Per Serving: Calories 160, Protein 2g

INGREDIENTS

1/2C dark chocolate, chopped

1/2C shredded coconut, optional

2T almond butter

2t vanilla

6T coconut oil, softened

2T maple syrup

1/2C chopped almonds

3T water

2C oats

1C almond meal

1/2t cinnamon

1/2t baking soda

1/2C brown sugar

pinch of salt

PROCEDURE

1.Preheat oven to 350 degrees. Put 1.5C oats in food processer with 3T water & pulse until flour-like. Add almond meal, cinnamon, baking soda & salt, pulse until combined.

2. Add coconut oil, sugar maple syrup, almond butter & vanilla until combined. Put dough in bowl, stir in remaining 1/2C oats, chocolate, coconut and almonds.

3. Scoop dough onto baking sheet lined with parchment paper. Bake 12 minutes until golden. Let cool 10 minutes. Yields 16-20 cookies. Enjoy!

Why did the cookie go to the doctor?

Because it was feeling crumbly!

Blueberry Oatmeal Muffins

Per Serving: Calories 145, Protein 3g

INGREDIENTS

1C quick oats	1C packed brown sugar
1C hot water	3/4C plain Greek yogurt
1/2C unsweet applesauce	1/4C olive oil
3C fresh or frozen blueberries	3 eggs
2C wheat flour	1/4t salt
1t cinnamon	1t baking soda
3t baking powder	1T vanilla

Blueberry
Oatmeal
Muffins

PROCEDURE

1. Preheat oven to 350 degrees. Combine oats and hot water in bowl, let sit 5-10 minutes.

2. In another bowl, whisk brown sugar, yogurt, apple sauce, oil, eggs and vanilla until smooth. Add baking poder, baking soda, cinnamon & salt. Whisk until smooth.

3. Add soaked oats & stir until blended. Add flour and berries, stir until combined. Don't overmix!

4. Grease muffin pan, fill 3/4 full. Bake for 20-25 minutes until a toothpick inserted comes out clean. Serve and enjoy!

Why did the blueberry break up with the muffin?

Because it was tired of getting mixed up in batter relationships!

Red Velvet Lava Cakes

Per Serving: Calories 212, Protein 16g

INGREDIENTS

3/4C red velvet cake mix   1t vanilla extract
pinch of sea salt   2T dark chocolate chips
4T granular stevia   2t dark cocoa powder
7T almond milk, unsweetened   1 egg
1T coconut flour   1t baking powder

PROCEDURE

1.Preheat oven to 350 degrees. Heat almond milk, dark chocolate, chips & vanilla extract in microwave in 30 second intervals until melted.

2. Add red velvet cake mix, dark cocoa powder, sea salt, stevia, coconut flour and baking powder to mix. Add egg and mix thoroughly.

3. Grease two ramekins, divide mixture evenly between ramekins. Bake for 12 minutes, cool for 5 minutes. Flip ramekins over onto a plate. Allow cakes to fall out to serve. Enjoy!

Red Velvet Lava Cakes

Spinach Muffins

Per Serving: Calories 76, Protein 2g

INGREDIENTS

3/4C milk
1C rolled oats
1t vanilla extract
2C baby spinach
1/4C honey
2 eggs
1t baking soda
1C wheat flour
1/8t salt
1C ripe bananas,
sliced
mini chocolate chips, optional
2T butter, melted or plain yogurt

Spinach Muffins

PROCEDURE

1.Preheat oven to 375 degrees, grease a standard muffin tin with non-stick spray. Place all ingredients exept flour & chocolate chips in a blender. Blend until smooth.

2. Add flour, pulse to combine. Pour batter in fto muffin tin filling 3/4 full. Sprinkle chocolate chips on top. Bake 11-13 mins or until firm to touch. Serve & Enjoy! Kids will love these too.

REMINDERS FOR HARD DAYS

WHOLE Hearted
SCHOOL COUNSELING

1. A bad day does not equal a bad life. *You are not this struggle.*

2. Not all thoughts are true. *Phew.*

3. Feelings are not facts. *But all your feelings are valid, real, and allowed.*

4. The only way out is through. *DARN IT.*

5. Your worth is not contingent on circumstances. *You are LOVABLE and ENOUGH always.*

6. Nothing stays the same. *Life guarantees this.*

7. You can't be everything to everyone. *But you can be true to yourself.*

8. Be gentle with yourself. And trust your inner voice, strength, resilience, and strength. *And be vulnerable.*

9. You're not alone. It's okay to ask for help. ∧

10. Focus on the things you can control. *Let go of the rest.* This is easier said than done.

Chocolate Chunk Cookies

Per Serving: Calories 148, Protein 2g

INGREDIENTS

1/2C butter, softened

1/2C sugar

1/2C brown sugar, packed

1 1/4C chocolate chunks

1/2t vanila

1/2t baking soda

1/2C rolled oats

1/2t baking powder

1/4t sea salt

1C flour

PROCEDURE

1.Preheat oven to 350 degrees, grease baking sheets. Combine butter sugar & brown sugar in bowl, beat with mixer until creamy. Beat in egg and vanilla.

2. Combine flour, salt, baking powder & soda in another bowl, mix well. Add flour mixture to butter mixture, beating continually. Stir in oats and chocolate chunks.

3. Drop batter by tspoonfuls onto baking sheets. Bake 8-10 minutes, until browned. Cool and put in airtight container until serving. Enjoy!

Chocolate Chunk Cookies

Carrot Cake Cupcakes

Per Serving: Calories 125, Protein 13g

INGREDIENTS

1/4C coconut flour

1/2C applesauce, unsweet

1/2C plain Greek yogurt

1/2t ground nutmeg

1t baking powder

1/2C egg whites

1t cinnamon

1t vanilla extract

1T honey

1C carrots, shredded

DID YOU KNOW?

Carrot cupcakes originated during World War II when sugar was rationed, and carrots were used as a natural sweetener. Today, they're loved for their moist texture and subtle sweetness, along with the added health benefits from carrots!

PROCEDURE

1.Preheat oven to 350 degrees. Place all ingredients in a bowl and mix well. Spray muffin pan or use paper cup holders and put the mixture in each tin. Yields 8-12, depending on how full you make them.

2. Bake for 15-20 minutes until toothpick comes out clean. Allow to cool 10 minutes.

3. Once they're cooled, frost each with cream cheese frosting. You can make homemade or use can frosting. Top with cinnamon, crushed walnuts or shredded carrots if desired. Enjoy!

Acai Blueberry Smoothy Bowl

Per Serving: Calories 398, Protein 23g

INGREDIENTS

3/4C plain Greek yogurt   1/4C coconut water
3.5oz frozen acai fruit puree   2T granola
1/2C frozen or fresh blueberries   1t chia seeds
1/2 medium banana, frozen   2T raspberries
2t toasted coconut flakes

PROCEDURE

1.Combine yogurt, acai blueberries, banana and coconut water in a blender. Puree until smooth.

2. Pour smoothie into a bowl and top with raspberries, granola, coconut and chia seeds. Serve cold & enjoy!

Acai Blueberry Smoothy Bowl

Food for thought

The emotional energy you carry when preparing a meal transfers directly into the food. This is why it is very important to never make a meal when you are in a bad mood. This energy transfer can either heal you or slowly poison you. Choose wisely.

INDEX

A

B

INDEX

C

F

INDEX

G

H

I

M

INDEX

INDEX

About the Author

Catarina's journey began in a quaint town of Monticello, Kentucky where the roots of her Southern charm and culinary prowess were firmly planted. At the age of four, she found herself under the wing of her grandmother, a culinary virtuoso celebrated throughout the town for her exceptional skills in the kitchen. Those early lessons sparked a lifelong passion for cooking and baking that has only intensified over the years.

Venturing into higher education, Catarina pursued her passion for communications and language at college, earning a degree in Journalism and Broadcasting. It was within this realm of writing that she discovered another avenue for self-expression and fell deeply in love with the art of storytelling.

Catarina's wanderlust led her to traverse the landscapes of Europe and America, immersing herself in diverse cultures and broadening her understanding of the world. Her affinity for both the written word and the culinary arts converged seamlessly when she embarked on the journey to publish her first cookbook, a culmination of her experiences, skills, and unwavering passion.

Beyond her creative pursuits, Catarina cherishes the joys of life, finding profound fulfillment in her role as a mother. Driven by a desire to share her love for both writing and cooking, she seeks to inspire others to savor the richness of these experiences. Her guiding philosophy, encapsulated in the mantra "Live Well... Eat Right...Find Your Light!" reflects not only her approach to life but also her sincere wish to spread positivity and delight through her words and recipes.

LinkedIn Link:
https://linkedin.com/in/catherine-medel-b07b9871

Facebook Link:
https://www.facebook.com/catherine.medel.5

Instagram Link:
https://www.instagram.com/catarinam_author

Made in the USA
Columbia, SC
19 May 2024

35507494R00089